Included also are two free bonus books (making this book a $20.85 value!) Your books are presented in this order:

1) Spanking Dictionary
2) Bare Bottom Spankings (The Las Vegas Adventure)
3) Bed Arrest, the Punishment for BDSM Enthusiasts

<u>Spanking Dictionary</u>

By Phil G.

Copyright (C) 2013

Books by Phil G include:

The Absolutely Essential Book of BDSM and S&M Rules
Things To Do During 3 Hours of Sex; A Step-by-step Guide
Playtime At The Dom Den; A Step-by-step Guide
The Absolutely Essential Guide to Great BDSM and S&M Sex
The Ultimate Collection of S&M and BDSM Rules For Female Submissives and Slaves
The World's Most Entertaining Kinky Personal Ads
Have Awesome BDSM Sex
The Funniest BDSM Personal Ads
BDSM Master/slave Contract
The Spanking Dictionary
BDSM Rules
Spanking Contract

The Spanking Dictionary

Caution is always advised in anything related to spanking, discipline and punishment. Always stay within legal boundaries.

Spanking pronouns, (which include names of spanking websites, spanking actors/actresses, spanking parties and spanking media) are NOT included in this dictionary due to space limitations. ***Spanking of minors is not discussed in this book nor advocated.***

ADULT SPANKING - Spanking taking place among and between people who are of legal age.

ADULT SPANKING SCENARIOS - Spanking activities that take place among adults. These are often thought up and set up ahead of time.

AMATEUR SPANKING – (1) Unless a person is spanking, or receiving spankings for money or other material gain (such as Spanking Therapists and professional FemDoms do,) then this category includes most in the adult spanking world. (2) While not all agree on this angle of the definition, it has been used to imply a spanker or spankee who is not proficient in the spanking arts.

ANAL EXAM – The dominant spends a lot of time inspecting, testing and ultimately using the spankee's anus for his/her pleasure.

ANGER MANAGEMENT THERAPY SPANKING - Spanking can be used as a kind of therapy to help manage anger. There are two different approaches.

(1) The angered/stressed person is the *spankee* and gets spanked for a length and an intensity that allows the anger/stress to be released. Multiple spankings may be needed.

(2) The angered/stressed person is the *spanker* and spanks for a length and an intensity that allows the anger/stress to be released. Multiple spankings may be needed.

ANNIVERSARY SPANKING - Like birthday spankings this involves a tradition where as part of the festivities one or multiple participants spank and/or get spanked. It may include a special sexual scenario also. Spankophiles might want to get creative and have these anniversaries occur on other anniversaries such as when the couple met, became engaged and/or had their first date.

AVERAGE SPANKING (An) – Your basic everyday spanking, the usual. (Yawn.)

BARE BOTTOM SPANKINGS – Applying the spanking directly to the uncovered buttocks.
There are advantages to this versus spanking the covered buttocks:

1) *Better access*; the spanker may wish to use the spankee's bottom for other types of stimulation including anal and vaginal stimulation. The spanker may want to rub the naked bottom sensually at various times, etc.

2) *Humiliation*; the spankee must expose him/herself.

3) *Intensity*; clothing can lessen the impact of the blows and thus lessen the spanking's sensation and/or ability to provide punishment.

4) *Safety*; All parties can see how the buttocks is fairing from the blows. Perhaps the intensity needs to be lessened; you might not know if the buttocks are covered.

BARE BOTTOM BEATING – See *Bare Bottom Spankings*.

BATHBRUSH – A long handled brush used for washing one's self during bathing. It can be an effective spanking tool.

BEDROOM TIME – Being banished to the bedroom after, and/or as part of a punishment spanking. Often this bad girl will get spanked more than once while serving bedroom time.

BED ARREST – A type of BDSM punishment. See *"Bed Arrest, the Punishment for BDSM Enthusiasts"*.

BEDTIME SPANKING – (1) Spankings irregularly administered as foreplay to sex prior to going to sleep for the night. (2) Spankings which are administered nightly (or irregularly) when the spankee and/or spanker goes to bed, whether there is to be sexual activity or not.

A number of spankees claim a bedtime spanking helps make them sleepy.

BEHAVIOR MODIFICATION SPANKING – Spanking(s) administered to change unwanted behavior. Repeated and hard spankings may well be necessary to make this work.

BELT – It holds a man's pants up and is a nasty spanking implement. You're in for it now young lady!

BIRCHING – Birching is to spank using a tied together collection of thin tree switches. A nice touch is to have the spankee go out and pick the tree switches herself and tie them together securely for future use or use as soon as it is made.

BIRTHDAY SPANKING - A "traditional" birthday spanking is given on the birthday of the spankee. The formula is to administer one swat for each year of age, plus one additional swat "to grow on, one to live on, one to be happy on, to get married on, etc." The last swat can be the hardest as it's for any bad behavior that he/she did last year.

Spankee beware! Many will say that each birthday party attendee gets to give the same number of spanks, which can make for hundreds of spanks!

The spankee might pick and choose who gets to do the spanking and birthday spankings are typically done clothed as it's often done at children's parties.

Birthday spankings are usually done by hand but if it involves consenting adults spanking that often won't be the case.

Dominants may want to incorporate "practice birthday spankings" with their submissives as another excuse to spank.

Birthday spankings can be given belatedly but typically are for only the spankee's previous birthday (not all his/her birthdays.)

Blindfolding the adult spankee might be a nice touch.

A *"Reverse Birthday Spanking"* is when the person having the birthday gets to give the spankings instead!

BOARD OF CORRECTION – Slang name for a paddle.

BOTTOMS UP – While more known as a saying for drinking everything from a glass (container) so the bottom of the container is pointing up (thus sending all the liquid into your mouth,) this also means presenting a bottom for a spanking.

BOTTOM RAKING - Sliding your fingernails over and across the spanked or unspanked ass. This should not be done hard enough to puncture the skin or even take any layers of skin off. This should also only be done over the fleshy part of the buttocks and not near the anus or sexual organs.

BROKE THE PADDLE ON MY BUTT – This saying can be put in different ways. It's a source of pride for the spankee that when someone spanked his/her butt using a paddle, the paddle broke upon hitting his/her butt.

BRUTAL SPANKING – See *Severe Spanking*.

CAPSAICIN CREAM – (Results vary from individual to individual.) - Applying a *very small* amount of this cream onto the naked buttocks is an alternative to spanking (thus is called *"Silent Spanking"*). It seeps into the bottom and often is painful. A surprisingly small amount is needed. Make sure to quickly wash your hands after applying it or you will be in pain too. (Better yet use something else to apply it with.)

Rub the *capsaicin cream* in well. It might take some time to make its impact well noticed. Spankers I suggest you first experiment by rubbing a tiny bit into your spankee's butt. Only drops of it would be necessary to first test his/her resistance to it. Olive oil or vegetable oil can help dissipate the pain. This cream may look innocent but the stuff is *evil*! (Tiger Balm is another possible punishment cream.) Do not put any of this on or in the anus or vagina!

CANING – This is when a cane is applied with force to the buttocks of the spankee. The cane can hurt more than many other spanking implements due to its smaller surface area so caution is advised. Also see *Switching*.

CARPET BEATER – A long handled housekeeping tool used to beat dust off of hanging rugs and to spank worthy bottoms.

CHARITY SPANKING - Charity Spanking is when people are spanked in exchange for others sponsoring them and giving money to one or more charities for each good spank they take. Also see *Professional Spanking*.

CLENCHING – (Clenching Cheeks) – This is when the spankee tightens his/her buttocks muscles together forcefully. This might be done in an attempt to dull the sting of the spanking.

COMING BACK IN FROM THE PUBLIC SPANKINGS – After the spankee returns to a private secluded setting, after having been in the public (and that includes having been to work or having been shopping), she gets a spanking as a natural course of events. This is over and above any other spankings she's getting for any other reason. This is associated with but the opposite of *Going Out in the Public Spanking*.

CONFESSIONAL {THERAPY} SPANKING - (1) A religiously related spanking scene where the spanker plays an authoritative person of religious faith who spanks the spankee in an effort to get him/her to be more religiously righteous or pay for his/her sins. This may be more popular in Domestic Discipline households. (This happened for real a lot more in centuries past than most hear about.)

(2) The spankee perhaps was raised in a strict religious environment and needs that type of strict (and perhaps regular) guidance to stay on the straight and narrow. A good spanking once or twice a week for just this could be a pleasant addition to your relationship. This obviously has similarities to the confessional of Catholics and doing penance.

(3) In an attempt to get the spankee to confess to something, he/she is spanked. Once he/she confesses then punishment would be administered, which would be another type of spanking such as *Punishment Spanking*.

CONFIDENTIAL SPANKING – The spanking partners agree to keep their spanking relationship and other spanking related activities secret, except to whom they both agree on. It is essential to follow this rule.

CONSENSUAL SPANKING – Informed and agreed-upon spanking that takes place between and among consenting adults.

CORPORAL PUNISHMENT – This is physical punishment inflicted on the human body. This includes spanking but can also include the death penalty.

CROP – A slapping instrument originally meant to urge horses to move. It can be a wonderful spanking implement.

CRUEL TO BE KIND – A saying that is loosely associated with the potentially beneficial impact of adult spanking.

DETENTION ROOM – This is where many naughty schoolgirls go in spanking films and fantasies. This is the location of much discipline, primarily spanking.

DISCIPLINARIAN – Someone with authority that dispenses discipline, often by giving spankings.

DISCIPLINE - It incorporates punishment to correct disobedience of the rules and/or other unacceptable behavior.

DIZZY SPANKING - For this kind of spanking, the spankee is spun around on foot or in a chair that can spin around, until he/she is dizzy. The spankee is then spanked. This is for healthy spankees only and it's essential to take care for safety.

DOMESTIC DISCIPLINE – (*Christian Domestic Discipline, Spanking for Jesus, Loving Domestic Discipline*) – This typically is discipline relegated for couples, and often is administered in Christian dominated households. Rules are instituted and penalties for disobedience are administered. The male tends to be the dominate person (*Head of Household* [HOH]).

DOMINATION SPANKING – The spanking often includes additional aspects of domination such as oral commands, punishment and physical restraint.

DROPSEAT PAJAMAS – These pajamas open at the buttocks for excreting waste and spanking.

DUEL SPANKING - (*Tandem Spanking*) - This is a *Spanking Contest* between spanking couples. The spanking is done simultaneous or one at a time. See *Spanking Contest*.

ENDURANCE SPANKING - This can be done to determine the spanking length and intensity limits of a spankee. (Of course limits change with time.) How much can the spankee take, how many swats, how hard can the swats be, how long can the spanking go on? Are there certain spanking implements that the spankee doesn't do as well with?

Spanking models often go through this unless they have good references.

ENEMA SPANKINGS – Combining enemas with spankings. The spankee is given a spanking then an enema is administered. The spankee releases the water and immediately gets another spanking.

EROTIC SPANKING - Erotic Spanking are spanking activities and techniques that are executed expressly to enhance sexual pleasure. Admittedly spanking (even the thought of spanking) likely enhances a spankopile's pleasure but with *Erotic Spanking* it's taken a step further. For instance the couple can alternate spankings with the use of a variety of sexual toys and/or manual sexual stimulation.

The spankee can be securely tied down so she/he is immobile and can be enjoyed in other ways after and in-between spankings.

EXERCISE SPANKING – If the spankee needs motivation to exercise and/or exercise harder, spanking can be of use. The spankee can be spanked whenever exercise goals are not reached and/or can get the more desirable reward of a pleasurable spanking when the goals are met.

EXHIBITION SPANKING – This is when spanking models, professional or amateur, provide the public with a spanking related show. The spankee(s) could be clothed or exposed. Also see *Public Spanking*.

EXORCISM SPANKING – ("Exorcism Beating") - This occurred historically in various places and times in both western and eastern orthodox Christianity, as well as in other religions. This also occurred as part of the inquisitions. In most cases however, the spankee was lucky if their main punishment was only being spanked (beaten.)

Over the centuries some clergy members, particularly those that still were allowed to have sex, set up chambers where women were spanked, sometimes on a sizable wooden cross, for their purported transgressions. It might have been just one spanking or a semi-regular occurrence.

The spankee's buttocks may or may not be exposed for the beating and onlookers may or may not be allowed to watch, or even aid in the beatings.

F/f SPANKING – Female spanking female.

F/m SPANKING - Female spanking male.

FIFTY SHADES OF GREY - A groundbreaking, famous 2011 erotic romance novel by British author E. L. James. Its erotic scenes include BDSM activities such as bondage, discipline, dominance/submission, sadism and masochism.

FIRM HAND – The spanker has a strong and likely big hand that can deliver impressively hard spanks.

FLOGGING – A flogger is a variation of the cat-of-nine-tails whip. It's typically made of suede or real leather and has many individual elastic strands attached to the handle.

GOING OUT IN THE PUBLIC SPANKING – Before the spankee goes out into the public (and that includes going to work or shopping), she gets a spanking as a natural course of events. This is over and above any other spankings she's getting for any other reason. This is associated with *Coming Back in from the Public Spankings*.

GOOD OLD FASHION SPANKING – These are the standard spankings we grew up with. *Silent Spankings* and many if not all spankings when the spanker is tied down to spanking furniture, likely are not in this category. This term denotes a hard or harder than normal spanking.

GROUP SPANKING – When a multiplicity of people conjugate for the expressed purposes of engaging in one or more kinds of spanking and spanking related endeavors.

HALLOWEEN SPANKING – Spanking on Halloween while people are in costume. Ideally the spankee(s) should not know who's doing the spanking. Another version has it that the spankee(s) are the ones that people can't tell the identity of.

HAIRBRUSH – (Hated Hairbrush) – The household hairbrush makes a very effective and surprisingly intense spanking tool. Mmmmmm!

HAND SPANKING – Directly applying the spanking blows to those naughty butt cheeks with your hand(s).

HANDPRINT – On a well spanked red ass, if the spanker lands a single hard spank, a white handprint on the otherwise red ass cheek might appear for a short time.

HARD SPANKINGS – A true spankophile should be able to take a hard spanking, at least from time to time. Hard spankings might only be relegated for punishment. Technically a hard spanking should not have the intensity of a severe spanking. Depending however on the pain threshold level of the spankee, a hard spanking could make a spankee cry.

Hard spankings however may evolve into your norm. You may find it best to tie down the spankee for a hard spanking.

The spanker can make demands of the spankee during a hard spanking, demands that need to be promised to be met before the spanking can stop. Perhaps by using a vibrator in her anus she would be required to cum before the spanking could stop.

Unless the spankee has very developed resistance, his/her bottom should be red and perhaps marked from a hard spanking.

If the spankee is female it's suggested that no hard spanking ever ends unless her pussy is wet just from the spanking and she's promising to be a very good girl!

HEATING PAD – (1) After a good spanking, if additional punishment is warranted, laying the heated pad over the well spanked buttocks might be the answer. (2) The spankee could place his/her butt on the heating pad before the spanking possibly making it more tender. (3) For some sitting on the heating pad can feel like punishment.

HOLIDAY SPANKING – Spankings in some cases can really add to the holiday cheer! (Of course there's always *Spanking Santa* in his red outfit!)

HOT SPANKING – Spanking that are more sexually stimulating than most.

HOUSE PADDLE – A paddle that is kept readily available as a courtesy for guests to use. (It can be another spanking implement instead and named accordingly).

HUMILIATION THERAPY SPANKING – Sometimes a person needs more humility, one way to give him or her more humility is to combine domination with long, hard spankings. Or just a long hard spanking could do the trick. Spanking Therapists and FemDoms can specialize in this.

ICE SPANKING – There are variations to this spanking technique. If you're interested you and your partner should experiment and find the way that works best for you.

The spankee will need to have her buttocks fully exposed. The spanker can do any of the following, or combine them:

a) First rub ice on/across her naked buttocks until the ice has melted. Dry the spankee's buttocks if so desired and administer a good spanking to the spankee.

b) After the first spanking is completed, start over with more ice and repeat this until you're done.

IF-THEN – This scenario can be used with adults, particularly in Domestic Discipline relationships. The number of spankings, spanking duration, intensity, length, implement used and number of spankings the spankee gets are set up ahead of time for a wide range of infractions. Over spending on a credit card would have a clear and previously defined punishment, as would being late for work etc. Couples can spend a lot of quality horny-time determining what punishments the submissive member of the relationship would get for which infraction.

IMPULSE SPANKING – Unexpectedly administering a spanking without warning and perhaps for no particular reason.

INSUFFICIENT DISCIPLINE – When the submissive party thinks (to him/herself, or out-loud) that the dominant is not disciplining him/her adequately or is strong enough emotionally to administrate the discipline.

JUICY BUTT – A bottom that likely is great for spanking (or one that someone thinks would be great for spanking.)

KNEADING (aka *Petrissage*) - The palms of the hands and/or fingers work the buttock's muscle and fat tissue. Kneading a spankee's bare buttocks is also popular before, during, and/or after a spanking.

KNICKERS DOWN – An English saying meaning "panties down" in preparation for the spanking she so desperately needs.

LEATHER BUTT - A slang term for buttocks that are comparatively insensitive to spanking and do not mark easily. With enough spankings many buttocks become less sensitive.

LESBIAN SPANKING – When women play with each other sexually, and that includes spanking.

LESBIAN SPANKING STORIES – Erotic girl-girl spanking literature.

LIMIT – The point where the submissive party is unwilling to accept any spanking related additional intensity, duration and/or experience.

LINGERIE SPANKING – Spanking while the pretty lady is wearing lingerie.

KISS OF THE PADDLE – When a blow from a paddle on the butt leaves a significant mark.

LAP-WRIGGLING SPANKING – (a.k.a. *Good Old-fashion Lap-wriggling Spanking*) – Wiggling while over a lap getting spanked. (This is more of an English term.) This wiggling likely is because the spanking is particularly intense or the spankee's ability to take a spanking is not too developed.

LIGHT SPANKING – This can be applied to a clothed or bare bottom. It can be administered by hand or via the use of a spanking implement. It should not be particularly painful for most spankees.

LONG, HARD SPANKING – A lengthy and intense punishment spanking meant to change unacceptable behavior.

MAINTENANCE SPANKINGS – (*Preventative Maintenance Spankings*) - Spankings administered on a regular basis to keep the spankee on the straight and narrow. Punishment spankings are administered in addition to these.

MARATHON SPANKING – Lengthy spanking sessions that might be part of spanking contest or simply for a couple to establish their own personal best. In some marathon spanking sessions the couple can take a short break periodically.

MARKS – (*Spanking Marks*) – A good spanking with more than moderate intensity (depending on how sensitive the spankee's bottom is) can leave the bottom a lovely shade of red. It also can leave light contusions and more significant bruises. These bruises (aka "marks") could remain for days or longer or they can be gone in hours. A spankophile is proud of these marks hence the phrase "wears her (his) marks with pride".

MEMORY RECOVERY SPANKING – Spankings administered to hopefully help the spankee remember things he/she had forgotten. The hope is that he/she can remember that forgotten thing while being spanked or afterwards.

M/f SPANKING – Male spanking female.

MODERATE INTENSITY SPANKING – A spanking administered with only moderate intensity typically will give the bottom some or more redness. It shouldn't make the spankee cry or leave marks. This all depends on how sensitive the spankee's ass cheeks are.

MOTIVATIONAL SPANKING – This type of spanking scenario can help the spankee reach their goals. Perhaps the goal is good grades in college, or weight loss, or quitting smoking. Motivational spankings can work (but like anything in life is not guaranteed to work.)

(1) Before the spankee embarks on their endeavor he/she can be given the first motivational spanking, which is a serious spanking that really show him/her that it's better to stick with the program. His/her subconscious mind needs to be motivated also and a really good spanking might do just that.

(2) Should the spankee fail to reach previously established goals, he/she should be very soundly spanked and otherwise punished. Other punishments can include corner time, not being allowed to wear cloths (when in private,) Bed Arrest, orgasm denial and other forms of humiliation can also be incorporated. Perhaps you'd also like to invite all your BDSM/kinky friends over to give him/her a spanking.

MUSICAL SPANKING – Spanking to the beat of the music and/or for the length of the musical composition. (Ever spanked to "Bolero"?)
Another great thing about music is that it might cover up the sound of the spanks hitting the spankee's bottom and noises the spankee utters as his/her bottom is reddened.

NAKED SPANKING – The spankee, and optionally the spanker, are not wearing any cloths.

NSA SPANKING – (No Strings Attached Spanking) – Casual spanking where a special relationship is not necessary.

OLD FASHIONED BARE BOTTOM SPANKING – These are the standard spankings we grew up with. *Silent Spankings* and many if not all spankings when the spanker is tied down to spanking furniture, likely are not in this category. This term denotes a hard or harder than normal spanking.

OTK – (a.k.a. *OTK Spanking*) – Short for *Over The Knee*. This is one of the most popular spanking positions. Its benefits include that the spanking can start quickly versus having to tie the spankee up. Also the spankee's private parts and ass, with all its features, are in easy reach for the spanker's use (assuming the spankee allows that.)

PADDLE – A rigid spanking implement that typically is quite a bit longer than it is wide. The thickness of a paddle can vary. Paddles can increase the intensity of the spanking blows and make spanking a less tiring affair for the spankers. Paddles are usually made of wood but can be made of other hard materials such as acrylic.

PARTY SPANKING – Spanking that takes place at social gatherings. This includes *Spanking Games* and *Group Spankings*. Party Spanking is not the same as *Spanking Parties*.

PLAYFUL SPANKING – This can be when the spankee gets only light to moderate swats or a limited number of quick swats. Consensual playful spankings might be used to break the tension.

POUTING - To make a facial expression that indicates dissatisfaction; sulking. This might be done by the spankee prior to the spanking or when there is an indication that a spanking will take place in the future.

PRIVATE SPANKING - These spankings are given in an isolated private setting with invited company only.

PREVENTATIVE MAINTENANCE SPANKING – See *Maintenance Spanking*.

PROFESSIONAL SPANKING – When money or material goods are exchanged for one or more spankings. Spankings are given professionally by *Spanking Theraphists, FemDoms, Spanking Demonstrators* and others. It could also be the opposite where it's the spanking model that gets spanked in exchange for money or material goods. (This includes spanking pictures and spanking video models.) *Charity Spanking* is when people are spanked in exchange for others giving money to one or more charities for each good spank the spankee takes.

PUBLIC SPANKING – (This includes *Exhibition Spanking*) – Spankings given in a public or semi public non-group spanking environment. (Not recommended!)

PUNISHMENT AGREEMENT – A *Punishment Agreement* is an oral or written agreement that defines what punishments will be given for what offenses. See *Spanking Contract* and *BDSM Contract*.

PUNISHMENT FETISH – The idea of being punished, or even of being punished in a certain way (such as being spanked) in some way turns on the individual and could be a re-occurring fantasy.

PUNISHMENT ROOM – A room, or area of a room (often the basement, bedroom or the dominant's study) where most of the spankings take place.

PUNISHMENT SPANKING - (*Discipline Spanking*) – These spankings leave the spankee's bottom red and marked. These are hard spankings meant to change a wayward spankee's behavior. Typically the female spankee (and sometimes male) will cry from these. Also applied as part of the punishment could be corntime, bedroom time and other punishments. Perhaps the spankee will only be allowed to crawl for the rest of the day/night if going somewhere in the house, (obviously privacy is required.) Maybe one punishment spanking will not be enough, or even two! The subconscious mind needs to know what he or she did is no longer allowed!

PURIFICATION RITUAL SPANKING – This spanking category is more on the spiritual side. It can combine enemas, massage, prayer, meditation and/or bathing for spiritual arousal and/or renewal.

PUSSY SPANKING – The vagina is lightly spanked for stimulation and/or punishment.

QUICKIE SPANKING – When time is limited, but the spankee must have a spanking, he/she can be bent over the nearest applicable furniture or go over your lap for an immediate spanking. Often this is when the spankee is already dressed for an occasion. A quickie spanking needs to be given instantly, likely without any significant preparation, waiting time, discussion, or scolding.

REAL TEARS – This indicates that what's occurring is a good hard spanking! Sometimes during a spanking video shoot, the spankee, in-between takes, has a bit of water put by her eyes to mimic tears. No need to do that when the tears are real!

RED BOTTOM SPANKING - (a.k.a. *Red Ass Spanking*) – A good spanking should leave the spankee with some or more redness on his/her bottom. A bottom that is covered with redness would be from a true *Red Bottom Spanking* that the spankee can 'wear' with pride! The red bottom may be accompanied with marks (bruises).

RELIGIOUS SPANKING – Religious spanking has a very long history. Men and women's buttocks have been beaten for, and by, religious authorities in many past civilizations. Certain members of Christian clergy are recorded to have spanked (women in particular) back when it was easier for them to get away with it.

Inquisitioners would beat men and women, often without mercy, as they considered them to be an affront to god.

A part of religious spanking history that may be of interest is how often women in the medieval and post medieval centuries, (often coupled women,) would request a spanking from the clergy (such as their minister or priest) as atonement for their sins or as confidential punishment for something isolated that they did. Often their husbands okayed it. Heck it was a lot better than going to hell right, at least that was what they thought.

Some church building basements had a separate section for these atonement sessions. This happened more often than people realize.

REWARD SPANKING – (1) When a spankophile just can't get enough spankings that you are actually able to reward her/him by giving a spanking. (2) A FemDom might consider all spankings she gives to her slaves to be a reward, or should be viewed as a reward. Punishment for bad behavior is typically more severe than a reward spanking.

ROMANCE SPANKING - This is for spanking couples involved in a romantic relationship. The spanking can be mixed with sexual stimulation and intercourse.

RULER – (Wooden Ruler) – Though often made of wood, it can be made of other substances. Some rulers are thicker than others and somewhat longer than one foot. The thick 1½ foot ruler is a dandy! The yardstick can be very useful for those long reaches, for instance when the naughty girl is sucking on a man's cock and he wants to spank her at the same time. (Watch out for those teeth!)

SAFE SPANKING – Don't spank too hard. Some spankees' butts are able to take more abuse than others, at least until the butt toughens up (assuming it does.) Also you want all parties to feel secure with the location and privacy of the place selected for the spanking.

SANDPAPER CHAIR – After the spankee is spanked, he or she sits naked on sandpaper. An alternative is to rub sandpaper on the spankee's well spanked bottom and/or run your fingernails over the spanked buttocks.

SCHOOLGIRL SPANKING – The naughty (adult) schoolgirl discipline fantasy is one of the most popular spanking fantasies. She is dressed in the pelted skirt and white dress shirt (perhaps also with a tie) and is constantly getting in trouble so she is constantly spanked! All female spanking enthusiasts (spankees) should have a schoolgirl outfit!

SELF-SPANKING – Spanking yourself.

SEXUAL DOMINATION – (Associated with *Sensual Domination*) - The dominant person controls and orchestrates the sexual relationship and sexual activity with the submissive person.

SERIOUS SPANKING – (1) Spanking enthusiasts that take the art of spanking seriously. (2) A hard or even severe spanking and typically is reserved for punishment.

SERVANT SPANKING – (Also see *Slave Spanking*) - Spanking of servants (though in past centuries and millennia they more often were slaves) occurred often. In those days masters and mistresses lorded over their servants with more power than they do today. If the lord (or mistress) of the house thought beating the servant would make good discipline (or simply enjoyed it), that was the servant's fate should she wish to continue working there, or often anywhere else as employment references were important.

The servant girl might be spanked for pleasure by the master of the house. She might be enjoyed in other ways too, though not as often from vaginal intercourse. Servant girls that ended up taking the role of concubines might be treated better and have less mundane work to do. Wives in those days were frigid move often than now. This might be because they were afraid to have too much sex with their husbands as it was so much easier to get pregnant back then thanks largely to a pronounced lack of birth control and the stricter demands of the prevailing religious forces that were staunchly against birth control. (Also women died during childbirth a lot more frequently back then.) A surprising number of wives simply considered the sex demands of their husbands to be too much and welcomed their use of a servant in that manner if it freed them from that arduous duty, (assuming he did not get her pregnant and kept his distance from her emotionally.)

The mistress of the house might order someone to be spanked (beaten) and perhaps do it herself. Husbands and male friends (or other servants) often were happy to do the beating for her, assuming it was a female getting spanked.

The person being beaten may or may not have the area being beaten, fully exposed (thus naked.)

SEVERE SPANKING - This type of spanking can cause much redness and/or severe bruising (marking), blistering or worse on the buttocks of most spankees. The spankee likely will find sitting a challenge for a certain amount of time. This needs to be done in a consensual manner and might not be legal.

SILENT SPANKING – (1) When the spankee is not allowed to utter any noise while being spanked. (2) Alternatives to spanking that quietly give the butt pain, such as the application of capsicum cream (but a very small amount) and the less effective Tiger Balm. Do not put it on the anus or sex organs.

SLAVE SPANKING – See *Servant Spanking*. (1) In the modern world of BDSM (*Bondage, Domination, Sadism and Masochism*) the submissive person is called a slave and is under the influence and/or control of the dominate party typically called the "Master" (if male) or "Mistress" if female. The submissive slave is dominated and spanked when the dominant feels it is necessary for discipline and/or pleasure. (2) (See *Servant Spanking* for more on this part of the definition.) Slaves in ancient times often were considered part of the family. They may have been expressly gotten for purposes of physical and sexual pleasure. They were spanked publically and privately in Roman and Greek locations at the whim of their owners. In the more modern slave ownership period including the Caribbean and in North America, black slave girls would also be used for sexual gratification when their owners wanted it. Also other male slaves might spank other slaves for various reasons, particularly when they were a supervisor.

SLIPPERING - Using a slipper as the spanking implement.

SOOTHING CREAM – (Cold Cream) - A cream applied to a well spanked bottom to limit the sensation of pain.

SOUND SPANKING – See *Hard Spanking*.

SPANKABLE – (Spankworthy) – The person is well suited to be spanked. They may appear to have an ass, due to its shape and/or appearance, that appears particularly well designed to be spanked. The mannerisms of the person should scream "spank me"! A professional spanking actress should have great "spankability".

SPANKED TO TEARS – When the spankee is spanked hard enough to cry real tears. Bad girl!

SPANKFEST – A synonym for "Spank Feast". This is a gathering, public or private, where spanking is one of the primary events (or at least is publicized to be.)

SPANKING ART - (Spanking Comics) – Spanking themed art.

SPANKING AGREEMENT - An oral or written agreement regarding spanking related activities. See *Spanking Contracts*.

SPANKING BEGINNERS – *Spanking Beginners* typically have little or no significant experience with giving a spanking and/or receiving a spanking.

It's important that the beginner's first spanking (or first few spankings) are as positive an experience as possible. Does the spankee want it to be a sexual experience also, if so then make sure sexual stimulation is accented. A bad experience now could turn this person off from spanking and another butt is lost to the spanking world :(

SPANKING BLOG – A (preferably) regularly updated online diary/web magazine that individuals and organizations keep regarding spanking pursuits.

SPANKING BONDAGE - When bondage is included with the spanking. Typically this means that the spankee is securely tied down and immobile for his/her spanking. Perhaps he/she is tied down to a piece of spanking furniture.

SPANKING CLUB – These associations provide a way to meet and/or otherwise intertwine with others in the spanking scene. They're sometimes called "Munches". Spanking clubs have grown quite a bit in number in recent years.

SPANKING CONTEST – When couples compete with spankings for a prize or prizes. The rules vary from contest to contest. Possibly included are:

A) Extra points for the spankee with the reddest butt
B) Extra points for the nicest looking marks
C) Points deducted for blistering or appearance of blood (typically then the spanking is over for them anyway)
D) Extra points for sexiest spankee's behavior while being spanked.
E) Points deducted for the spankee trying to block blows or get away
F) Points deducted for the spanker tiring too quickly
G) Extra points for the spankee with the sexist outfit and/or the outfit most conducive to making the spanking easier
H) Extra points for the spanker/spankee couple that is the most fun to listen to during the spanking
I) Extra points for how sexy and submissive the spankee is during and at the end of the spanking. She will have to beg for forgiveness, etc.
J) Extra points to the couple that uses the most spanking implements during the spanking

K) Extra points to the spankee's bottom that feels the best after being well spanked.

L) Extra points to the spankee that gets the most aroused

M) Extra points for the spankee with the most spanks during that time period.

Multiple spankings can be going on at the same time. Also see *Duel Spanking*.

SPANKING CONTRACT - It's a good idea for the participants to sit down and talk about their spanking scenarios, including under what circumstances the spanking will take place, how the spanking will be delivered, number of swats, instruments to be used, position of the person to be spanked, whether spanked with clothing on or bare bottom, etc. All participants then have an oral agreement on the terms, or have a signed written contract on the terms. This author sells a *Spanking Contract* through your ebookstore.

SPANKING CURRENCY - This is when spanks take the place of money, more specifically in place of your country's currency. How many spanks do you have in your spanking account? What are you going to buy with them? Or perhaps you are making a trade? Do you have a debt to pay off?

A common "spanking currency" scenario is paying off a debt. The spankee gets spanked in exchange for the debt.

SPANKING DANCE –The sub/slave does a sexy dance in front of her dominant and is spanked at various parts (times) of her dance. Perhaps it's after the end of each song, or if her dancing is not of an acceptable nature.

SPANKING DEMONSTRATION - When spanking partners demonstrate various aspects of spanking, including spanking implements and the best ways to spank.

SPANKING ENTHUSIAST – (Spankophile) - Someone who enjoys spanking, either receiving or giving. This includes activities related to spanking such as spanking media, building spanking furniture and spanking modeling.

SPANKING FANTASY – (Spanking Fantasies) – Mental images that run through one's head associated with spanking. A great many people have these.

SPANKING FOR COUPLES – Adult spanking activities that couples involve themselves in.

SPANKING FURNITURE – These apparatuses are used to place and secure one or more spankees. These include whipping benches, the spanking horse, the birching horse and the spanking bench. The spankee may or may not be tied down to it. The spankee often will find him or herself in the kneeling position or bent-over position. There should be easy access to their buttocks and often spanking furniture make the buttocks the most elevated portion of the spankee's body. Also being able to take and/or play with the spankee sexually while on and/or tied to spanking furniture is of pronounced importance.

SPANKING GAMES – (1) Online interactive games where the players determine who gets spanked and the intensity of the spankings. A spanking game may let the player interactively spank one or more characters. (2) Physical games such as Strip Poker that calls for one or more participants being spanked at various intervals. This type of spanking game typically has a way of determining who the spankee is and who the spanker is.

SPANKING HOST – The host or hostess at spanking social events and online and real-life spanking clubs.

SPANKING IMPLEMENTS – These physical devices are used to aid and enhance the delivery of the spanking blows. Examples include paddles, straps, slappers, floggers, rods, switches, canes, spanksticks, crops, the tawse and whips. Not everybody agrees but some people feel this category also includes restraint aids such as handcuffs and rope.

SPANKING LIFESTYLE – The world of spanking is innately intertwined into the lives of the spanker and/or spankee.

SPANKING MAGAZINE – Content from these wonderful periodicals now are often also online.

SPANKING MASSAGES – Combining full or partial body massages with spankings. The massaging may be the primary activity or vice versa.

SPANKING MASTURBATION – (1) Masturbating during and/or after a spanking and masturbating on those days afterwards while your bottom is still sore from the spanking. (2) Being spanked for masturbating.

SPANKING ORGASM – An orgasm that is obtained while one is being spanked, or while their buttock is still smarting from having been spanked in hours or days since the spanking.

SPANKING PARTY – Spanking parties might be in a home, a hotels or resort and are a gatherings specifically set up to accommodate spanking. Often there tends to be a significantly higher percentage of males at these events than females.

SPANKING POSITIONS – The bodily location of spanker and spankee just prior to, during and just after the spanking.

SPANKING PRACTIONER – See *Spanking Enthusiast*.

SPANKING REMINDER – This often is a short but relatively intense spanking session to make sure the spankee remembers to be obedient and/or is reminded as to what kind of punishment awaits her should she do something wrong.

SPANKING ROLEPLAY - There are many role-play scenarios that can include spanking. Naughty nurse, submissive maid, naughty schoolgirl, misbehaving cheerleader and warden/prisoner role playing is popular with male dominants and female submissives.

Spanking Roleplaying can require acting and props but it always includes a generous helpings of spankings.

SPANKING SERIES – A sequence and/or collection of spankings and/or spanking characters, stories, videos and/or pictures, which have certain characteristics in common.

SPANKING SESSION – Most associated with visits to FemDoms and Spanking Therapists. These are often "visits" that have a purpose but it still can be just a girlfriend and boyfriend meeting for fun.

SPANKING STICK – These look a lot like manmade canes.

SPANKING STORIES – (*Spanking Novels, Spanking Novellas, Spanking Series, Corporal Punishment Fiction, Flagellation Erotica, Romantic Spanking Stories*) – These are literature adventures involving spanking. These go back to the 1700s and may or may not involve sexual activities. The Marquis de Sade is among the most famous of these authors. In the past these tended to be clandestine publications that were sold secretly.

SPANKING THERAPIST – A person that administers *Spanking Therapy*.

SPANKING THERAPY – This aims to help spankees improve themselves. Perhaps he/she needs more motivation or just the tension release of a good spanking. The spanking is conducted by a professional. The spankee's needs are assessed and addressed in a controlled, nurturing environment (assuming nurturing is what the spankee wants.)

SPANKING VIDEOS – Spanking videos have proliferated with the Internet. As is obvious, these videos show spankees getting spanked and often dominated in other ways.

SPANKING WITH **ANAL STIMULATION** – (1) Directly stimulating the anus while giving a spanking (which can include aiming the blows at the anus and/or to make the blows include the anus.) It can occur before a spanking, and/or in between spankings, and/or after a spanking. This might involve inserting a butt plug (inflatable or otherwise), finger(s), anal vibrator, a dildo, or rectal thermometer into the anus. It might include carefully spanking a dildo that's already put into the anus to make it move up and down in the anus as blows are applied to it and the buttocks. (2) Actually spanking the anus with a narrow spanking instrument. (Spanking related enemas are a separate subject, see *Enema Spanking.*

Anal stimulation doesn't necessarily include anal intercourse.

SPANKING THE MONKEY – Male masturbation.

SPANKOPHILE – – (*aka Spanking Enthusiast*) - Someone who enjoys spanking, either receiving or giving. Their interest could also include spanking implements, discussing spanking, spanking media, building spanking furniture and spanking modeling.

SPENCER SPANKING PLAN – A well known domestic discipline spanking contract that originated in the 1930s.

STING AND THUD - Thinner spanking instruments such as switches release their energy closer to the skin and thus 'sting' more. Thicker spanking instruments such as paddles release their energy down further in the buttocks making more of a "thud" sensation.

STRAP – (aka *Leather Strap*) – A spanking instrument of various sizes that can be deliciously effective. It's often made of leather and thus is pliable.

STRESS RELIEF SPANKING – (*Tension Relief Spanking*) - The aim of these spankings are to eliminate frustration and guilt and cleanse oneself mentally. At the conclusion of these spankings relaxation and comfort can be had by the spankee.

STRUGGLING – When the spankee fails to hold his/herself adequately in place for/during and after their spanking.

SUBMISSIVE SPANKING – When the spankee wants to feel dominated as part of the spanking, over and above the domination involved with him/her getting spanked.

SUBMIT AND OBEY – A Dom/sub lifestyle outlook where the submissive submits and obeys his/her Dominant.

SWITCH SPANKING – Where the spanker and spankee take turns spanking each other.

SWITCHING – (Associated with Birching) – A switch is a flexible thin branch (rod) from one or more trees. (A collection of thin branches can be tied together to also be used as a spanking implement.) A switch is applied with force to the buttocks of the spankee. The switch like the cane can hurt more than many other spanking implements due to its thinner surface area so caution is advised. Also see *Caning*.

TENDER – The tendency for the buttocks to become sensitive to the touch after a good spanking.

TENSION RELIEF SPANKING – See *Stress Relief Spanking*.

THRASHING – This term is more popular in England and denotes a hard spanking/beating often with one or more implements.

TICKLE SPANKING – (1) Tickling the buttocks and then spanking it (an act that can be repeated.) (2) Tickling various parts of a person's body such as their belly and the bottoms of their feet, and also spanking that person's buttocks, alternatively or simultaneously.

TIT WHIPPING – Spanking the breasts of a woman using one or more implements. This can only be done consensually and with caution.

TRADITIONAL SPANKING – This denotes standard methods of spanking. No unusual methods of buttocal pain infliction, such as *Silent Spanking*, would be included in this category.

TOP UP SPANKING – These are given regularly, even every few days, even in addition to any other spankings the spankee has received. These spankings are for bad behavior that the spankee got away with during that time period (say week) and for bad behavior she might be tempted to do in the following week. See *Maintenance Spanking*.

TOUCH-YOUR-TOES – When in a standing position the spankee may be ordered to reach down and touch as close to their toes (perhaps their knees) as possible so their buttocks can tighten and stick out thus becoming an easier target to spank.

TOUGHEN-UP SPANKING – These spankings (and spankings in general) if given with regularity, can dull nerve endings in the buttocks as well as toughen tissues in the buttocks. The spankee might evolve into having a "leather butt" which is a butt that can take a disproportionately hard spanking.

WAKE-UP SPANKING – This well helps to wake up sleepy beauty and typically works much better than an alarm clock.

WARM-UP SPANKING - This is a light spanking, often by hand and perhaps on a clothed bottom, before the "real" and more intense spanking begins. Its purpose is to prepare the butt for the coming onslaught.

WEARS HER (HIS) MARKS WITH PRIDE – (*Spanking Marks*) – A good spanking with more than moderate intensity (depending on how sensitive the spankee's bottom is) can leave the bottom a lovely shade of red. It also can leave light contusions and more significant bruises. These bruises (aka "marks") could remain for days or longer or they can be gone in hours. A spankophile is proud of these marks hence the phrase "wears her (his) marks with pride".

WEIGHT-LOSS SPANKING – If the spankee needs motivation to lose weight, spanking can be of use. The spankee can be spanked whenever weight loss goals are not reached and/or can have the more desirable reward of a pleasurable spanking when the goals are met. Perhaps the spankee should be given a hard spanking just before the diet is to begin to remind him/her what's in store if transgressions occur.

WELL-SPANKED BUTT – A buttocks that has the tell-tale signs of having gotten a good spanking.

WET SPANKING – For this the spankee's butt is made wet. It can also be when the spankee wears something wet that covers her bottom and is spanked over that. This can enhance the pain coefficient.

WHEEL BARROW SPANKING POSITION – The spanker sits up and the spankee lays her hands on the floor directly in front of the spanker. The spankee spreads her legs and brings her ass and legs up over the sitting spanker's lap. Her legs are positioned on each side of his upper torso. Her pussy and anus are spread wide open next to his midsection. Her ass cheeks are on his lap, her spread open pussy lips are facing him.

WHEEL BARROW SPANKING – When the entire spanking is administered with the spankee in the wheel barrow spanking position (see previous definition.)

WHUPPIN – Slang for whipping.

WOODEN SPOON – This kitchen implement can also double as a spanking implement. Bad girl!

End

These books are sold and/or distributed with the understanding that the publisher and author is not engaged in rendering legal or other professional services. **These books and its subject matter are for entertainment purposes only.** In these publications there may be inadvertent inaccuracies including technical inaccuracies, typographical inaccuracies and other possible inaccuracies. **The writer and publisher of these publications expressly disclaim all liability for the use or interpretation by anybody of information contained in these publications.** The author, publisher and distributors of these publications hereby disclaim any and all liability for any loss or damage caused by errors or omissions resulted from negligence, accident, or any other causes. If legal advice or other expert assistance is required, the services of a competent professional person in a consultation capacity should be sought. Products, services and websites' content vary with time. Please verify any published information.

Bare Bottom Spanking

By Jim Rollins

Copyright (C) 2013

I want to tell you about an incredible spanking adventure I treated myself to in 2009.

My company temporarily transferred me to Las Vegas, a city in the midst of a terrible recession.

I had hoped to meet some kinky ladies to play with, in particular to spank on their bare bottoms, but when I talked to them in casinos and bars, too often they ended up being sex workers (prostitutes) versus eligible single ladies so finally I decided to just go with it.

I put aside $1,000 and planned on spending it all on spanking call girls on their bare bottoms, (and any sex that came along with it.)

I put a few ads online explaining that she would give me a massage, then I could play with her as I wished and she would get spanked good and hard on her bare bottom. Her butt would be red and marked and any girls that couldn't handle it need not apply. I even asked for pictures of their previously well spanked butts as reference. I also told them to expect their hands to be tied together as this spanking would hurt.

I would pay each sex worker $200 cash. Happily I was gifted with many inquiries from the ads. Allow me the pleasure of telling you more about them.

1. September 17th, Wendy - This shapely brunette was "kinky", 5'4" and 135 pounds according to her online advertisement. As she wouldn't verify online or on the phone how much of a spanking she could take, I met her at a casino bar and we talked for a while. She sure was cute. Her top was cut so low her breasts threatened to fall out when she walked. She was dressed as a sex toy and I sure hoped this was going to work out as my little man downstairs was real interested in her.

A neat thing about meeting a sex worker at a bar in preparation for playtime is that you got to socialize with a (hopefully) fine looking lady, though not for long if things didn't work out. This time however it did.

I showed her pictures of well spanked girl's bare bottoms and told her that is what she should expect. She asked for more money (this would happen often with the girls.) I politely refused. She finally agreed and insisted she could handle it.

We went back to my place. She freshened up in the bathroom, came out and stripped. (I had the $200 on top of the TV.) Her butt was a bit loose but very spankable. Her tits were firm and lovely (she later said they were recently enlarged.)

I was on the couch. She knelt down in front of me and said she was ready to do whatever I wanted. As I was also naked I thought what the heck and told her to suck on my cock. Hmmmm that was a good move too! She sucked like a pro and I was hard in a jiffy, however I was here to start my spankfest as I just had to have this monster spanking memory to look back on when I was old and gray.

As tough as it was to pull myself away from her surprisingly strong mouth, I did. I told her to get my bag of spanking implements and put it on my right side. With her eyes wide open she said something like "wow you're prepared." I ordered her to once again to kneel in front of me and I tied her hands together.

Well the time had come. I told her to lie over my lap with her head on the left.

Spending a little time massaging the delicate bare bottom that was about to get roasted seemed only fair, as well as teasing her pussy with the vibrator. She clearly enjoyed both, particularly the later.

I put the vibrator down and pulled out a black 12 inch long leather slapper, resting it on her butt, making her moan in anticipation. "You know what to expect young lady. Now stay in place or it will only get worse."

"Yes Sir" she meekly said, fidgeting.

I lifted the slapper up and *Whack! Whack! Whack! Whack!* I spanked her lovely bare bottom with precision, this was going to be a long night for it and I wanted to make every inch of it red. Yes 'redness' was tonight's key word!

WHACK! WHACK! Smack! Smack! SMACK! She started moaning and breathing deeply. "Ow that hurts!"

"Well it's supposed to hurt young lady." I reminded her. SMACK! SMACK!

She tensed as she wondered what was now to come, then she began yelping regularly as she felt the slapper repeatedly come down hard across the curve of her bare bottom. She regained her breathing as I temporarily rested the slapper on her butt. She then felt the slapper lift off her posterior and she heard it whistle through the air as it came down again on her vulnerable ass, time and time again. She was now crying out with each strike and reeling from the barrage of blows. I then stopped and exchanged the slapper for a paddle to continue her spanking. The paddle would make her squeal and kick her feet. The spanking continued.

After what felt like an eternity to her I stopped and she flinched while I rubbed her reddening butt. "This looks great" I said impressed as her bare bottom was reddening nicely. "Imagine what your ass is going to look like when were done....Lucky girl!"

SMACK! SMACK! SMACK! She yelled as she felt the paddle come down on her ass again and again, "Please sir just use your hand" she begged. No way I thought, that was not part of the bargain. *WHACK!* That felt harder she thought and indeed she was right, I had exchanged paddles, this was a bigger one. Well at least it wasn't a cane she thought. She hated the cane. But still, knowing that it wasn't the cane didn't lessen the pain of the spanking. She yelled each time it struck. I counted fifty new blows on her hot, red, marked bare bottom before it stopped. What a sight she was, crying and kicking her feet like a naughty schoolgirl.

I stopped to admire the view. This was indeed a great memory in the making.

"Please stop, oh please sir!" she begged.

"Are you going to be a good girl?" I asked firmly. "Yes sir I promise" she responded submissively. I wanted to let her go right then but I wanted my money's worth of bare bottom spanking. Yes one more volley on her red, marked bottom would do the trick.

Slap! Spank! BAM! Slap! Crack! Spank! Bam! I spanked down her upper legs but stopped fearing that the redness on her legs would show out in the public as she was wearing such a short dress. Instead I went back to paddling her upper and outer bare bottom as those regions weren't as red. SMACK! SMACK! SMACK! The crying she had started a while back was making her even more sexy. This was really a great way to start my Las Vegas spanking memory.

Well the spanking finally ended and I let her down to kneel in front of me. Her hands were still tied so she couldn't rub her red well spanked bare bottom that well even though she desperately wanted to. I would do that for her instead. It was hot and a lot of fun to rub. I was holding her close as I bent down to rub her red, marked bare bottom and rake it with my fingernails. She was still snifling.

"Suck on my cock young lady and drink down all my cum. If even a drop is lost we start your spanking all over again." "Oh god no" she begged and eagerly started sucking on my cock with her tied hands massaging my balls. Soon I would cum and true to her word she drank down every drop of my cum.

She would call me again periodically asking if I wanted another session but she insisted on more money so it never happened.

2. September 24th, Jennifer - Jennifer was actually the first to answer one of my online ads but after I responded back to her, I didn't hear from her for 9 days. She had insisted that she was a spankophile and "could suck every drop of cum out of me." Oh course she wanted more money but eventually agreed to the $200 as money was so tight in the recession.

Since we had talked on the phone (and I even had her smack her own bottom with a ruler many times while on the phone to prove she meant business,) I decided to just let her come over. Later that night the door bell rang and even though I was only wearing a bathrobe, I let her in. She took the money and put it in the purse. We talked a bit and I gave her a drink to loosen her up. She then pulled out a leather strap from her bag and asked me to only use that on her. I agreed.

Jennifer had long red hair and nice tits with cute little nips. Her best feature though was her round, tight ass. It looked like it was begging to be spanked. She told me how she loved to feel the sting of the blows and the jiggling of her bare bottom which she could feel all the way up her spine. She said a good hard spanking impacts all her sexual points, her nipples get hard like little pencil erasers, her pussy juice starts dripping down her inner thighs, and her asshole quivers. A big cock, spankings and my red ass cheeks that come along with it, really gets me off she said in the sexist way.

Well that description had come out of the blue and sure left my cock hard. I got the impression on the phone that she was into being spanked but this was even more than I expected. I removed my bathrobe and presented her with my newly hardened cock. Her eyes had been transfixed with my midsection since she walked in and seeing my big, hard cock made her quickly strip. I particularly liked seeing her see-thru pink panties. She knelt down in front of me and began sucking on my little man with a vengeance.

I reached down and played with her tits. My cock generously provided her with copious amount of ooze, which she lapped up as she softly moaned. I then reached over her back and played with her cute tight ass. She must work out as it was so firm.

Oh oh, I was about to cum so I lifted her head off my cock, put her hands together on my lap and tied them together as she shuddered with anticipation. She was really turned on now, her heart was beating fast partly out of nervousness and partly out of lust.

"Spread your legs as far as you can and keep your eyes on my cock" I told her as she was kneeling in front of me, soaking wet. I reached down to her pussy and spent some quality time playing with her clit. It took very little to make her cum, however it wasn't for near as long as she would have preferred.

I then told her to lie over my lap and Las Vegas spanking number 2 began.

Smack! Smack! Smack! I used my entire hand on her ass cheeks making it land repeatedly right on the fleshiest part...SMACK! SMACK! SMACK!

I was in a blissful state of ecstasy after giving her 40 hard blows. I pulled her ass cheeks apart and slide 2 fingers in and around her pussy just to tease her. I know she needed to cum again. I know she wanted to squirt all over my lap right then and there to relieve the tension in her aching pussy. But no way would I allow that.

But now back to the business at hand. I renewed my vigor and spanked her bare bottom harder. Jennifer went from moaning loudly to crying out as the blows came down hard and heavy. *WHAP! WHAP! WHAP! SMACK! SMACK!* Her ass cheeks had reddened quickly. One never knows who's ass will reddened the fastest. "Your ass reddens quickly, I like that" I said still spanking. She just moaned loudly, no doubt wishing I'd take a vibrator to her pussy.

SMACK! SMACK! SMACK! The leg kicking had gone into full swing now. It was fun to watch. It didn't slow down my spanking though. BAM! BAM! "Oh please stop" she half heartedly cried out. I knew how that goes thought, she didn't want it to end at all.

Hmmm the lower ass cheeks weren't as red as the middle so paddling there became the latest order of business. *WHACK! WHACK! WHACK!*

"Please fuck me, oh god please fuck me" she begged as I continued in my spanking quest. *BAM! BAM! BAM!*

"Beg for my cock in your pussy, beg for it slut!" I bellowed still spanking her red ass hard. *SMACK! SMACK! SMACK! SMACK! SMACK!*

"Please, fuck me, fuck my red, beaten ass!"

Well fucking her well spanked butt was an unexpected request but man was I ever ready for that.

"I will keep spanking your bare bottom until I don't have any energy left, or I can stop and fuck you right now in your ass, which would you prefer young lady?" "Oh god yes fuck me in my ass now please" she pleaded.

And that was that, another spanking in the books. I let her off my lap with her hands still tied together. I told her to get on the bed. I quickly got some petroleum jelly, a small towel and a condom.

She was on her elbows and knees with her swollen pussy lips facing me. I could see pussy juice dripping off of her. I got on the bed behind her and lubed her ass generously with my finger. I then wiped my finger off, put the condom onto my already hard cock and looked down at her red ass with delight wondering what she was thinking.

Jennifer had felt the prodding and lubing of her asshole stop, only now it was replaced by the feeling of my cock pressing into her little ass opening. She knew it would hurt a little but she loved to be fucked in the ass, even if it hurts at first. I slowly stuck it in, pressing past her sphincter and thrusting all the way inside. Her asshole stretched to accommodate my cock.

"Mmmmmmmmmm!" She let out a moan as I pressed into her. She was ready to cum. She wanted me so badly to touch her pussy, or for her to even just to rub it with her bound hands, then, unable to wait any longer, using her bound hands, she played with her clit, screaming out as she came.

With a big thrust my dick was inside her ass. I started thrusting slowly but worked my way to thrusting into her fast and hard. She let go and came with abandon.

Well that was definitely a memorable spanking experience but like all good things it came to an end. Jennifer spent the night, we had breakfast out the next morning and she went her way, though would call periodically.

3. September 30th, Tiffany – Tiffany knew Wendy, the first sex worker I spanked. Wendy told her of my spanking quest and she was anxious to join in the fun, and make some money!

We talked on the phone but I didn't hear from her for a few days. Suddenly one night I get a call and she is wondering if she could come over right then and there for her spanking. I said sure! When she got there however she first asked if she could take a shower. Perhaps that was to clean off the smell of the other johns. I said sure. She was in there around 20 minutes. Spanking memory number 3 was about to begin.

I told her not to bother getting dressed after she showered. I had undressed myself and laid all the sex toys and implements out, (as well as the $200.)

Through the closed door of the bathroom I said that she was a bad girl for taking too long with her shower and she was going to get a good spanking.

She came out, naked and looking very excited. She looked at me real seductive like and said "Have I been a bad girl? Are you going to spank me?"

"Yes young lady you have been a bad girl and you're going to get a good spanking."

Tiffany was curvy. She weighed about 150 pounds and had C-cup breasts. They hung down a bit but were still nice. She clearly was very turned on.

"You've needed a good spanking for sometime haven't you young lady?" "Yes sir" she said, her eyes fixed on my hardening cock.

"I'm going to bend you over this chair and I'll spank your ass good and hard for being a naughty girl."

All she could do was hang her head and stare at the floor. Her pussy was so wet that she had pussy juice running down her thighs.

"Answer me slut." I commanded.

"Yes..." She stammered now as she was confused as to how she got so turned by all this so fast.

"Yes what slut?"

"Yes sir." She replied quickly.

Her clit was throbbing, so she started to rub it. "Don't you dare touch yourself without my permission young lady" I quickly said. "Please may I touch myself sir" she begged.

Without answering I went over and grabbed her hands pulling her over the back of the chair. I tied each hand to different chair legs, then stopped and looked at my handiwork.

She looked scared like maybe she was concerned I was a weirdo and she had gotten herself in too deep.

"Don't worry Tiffany, you are not in any danger but you're going to get one heck of a spanking!"

That made her feel better and she said "Yes sir I'm a naughty girl. I need to be spanked. I want to be spanked. Spank my bare ass Sir."

"Say it again, and say it louder."

"Yes sir, I'm a naughty girl, I need to be spanked, I want to be spanked. Spank my bare ass Sir" she said trembling as she stared at the carpet.

As she was submitting so readily to me I decided to lube up her anus, maybe I'll take her in it after her bare bottom spanking. I could see that her nipples were rock hard. She looked up at me and saw that I was staring right at them. As I lubed her ass with a dildo she looked back and watched, moaning with pleasure. She also saw that my cock was already hard.

It was time. I then walked behind her and started to spank that lovely bare bottom. *WHACK! WHACK! WHACK! WHACK! WHACK!* Red hand prints appeared on her ass as she let out sexy yelps with each blow. SMACK! SMACK! SMACK! SMACK! SMACK! "Hmm, nice ass" I said and kept spanking her. *"Oww, ohhhhhh, ahhhhh"* was her reply. Still it was clear that she was loving it as she began pushing her ass out to meet my hand.

My hand flew up and down, crashing down again and again on her firm bare bottom. I gave her around 60 hard swats when I noticed sweat was forming on my brow. My arm was also starting to tire. No problem, I have another arm and I went to her other side so I could use my left arm instead. BAM! BAM! BAM! BAM! *"Ohhhh please owwwwwww"* was all she could say.

"Let's see how wet you are slut" I took a break and reached down between her ass cheeks, feeling for her pussy. I pushed one, then two fingers deep in her pussy. She lifted her head and moaned with pleasure. "Wow are you ever a wet little naughty slut that likes being spanked and is hungry for some cock. I bet you want it up the ass right now, don't you?

"Yes." she stammered, her face burning with shame and excitement. Stealthily I grabbed a paddle.

"Yes what?" I said punctuating the question with the paddle.

WHACK! *"Owwwwwww"*

"YES SIR!" She replied. The sting of the spanking had spread to her pussy; the sharp blows of the paddle were leaving an impression. Oh how that paddle burned her ass and yet she still pushed her ass back for more. She wanted more, she wanted to be paddled like the naughty slut she was. She also wanted desperately for his big cock to be in her mouth, her pussy, her ass.

"Yes sir what?" He asked again, spanking her more and hard with the paddle. *WHACK! WHACK! WHACK!*

"*Yes sir I want your cock in my ass.*" She cried.

Well I had been spanking her for around 15 minutes and her ass was beet red. Clearly this was a good spanking but I longed to use the paddle more on her, and that's what I did.

WHAP! WHAP! WHAP! SMACK! The paddling went on and on bringing a big smile to my face. She was crying and begging for it to stop. After another quick 20 more swats, the spanking was over.

I reached down and tied each of her feet to their respective feet of the chair. She squirmed some but I was too strong and she wasn't in a good position to do much. She now had her hands and legs tied down to the chair. I then came around her front and stuck my cock in her eager mouth. She sucked on it for all she was worth. "Suck hard young lady or I start your spanking all over again."

I stayed there getting my cock sucked hard, though it was a tough thing for her to do with her hands tied and her upper torso hanging over the chair, still she knew better not to do a good job sucking.

As nice as her sucking was it had come time to take her on the other end. I pulled out of her mouth, dried my cock off and put on a condom. I went to her backside and quickly rammed my cock deep in her soaking wet pussy, fucking her for all I was worth.

"*Oh god yes!*" She cried out as he filled her pussy with his hard cock. She began pumped my cock as much as the ropes would allow.

I reached under her and fingered her clit knowing it would send her over the edge. "*Yes! Yes! Yes!*" she cried.

It was great to feel her pussy contract around my cock as she came again and again.

But she still had a nicely lubed ass left to fuck and I wasn't going to let that opportunity pass me by. I pulled out of her pussy (to her objection) and entered her ass, soon cumming hard with a shout.

Well that was another great spanking and fucking session. Dang Las Vegas can be a fun town.

4. October 7th, Cindy - Cindy was another working girl that knew one of the girls I had already played with. I talked to her several times as initially I got the impression she was not sure if she wanted to be spanked. Actually I had given up on her when she called and insisted we do it. I wasn't convinced and actually I was the one that refused. Then one night, out of nowhere, Wendy (who I had already spanked) called and said she was bringing Cindy over and that I could do whatever I wanted with her, for the $200 of course. (I would later find out that Cindy owed Wendy money and needed cash fast which is why I was supposed to pay Wendy and not her.)

Wendy also wanted to know how well Cindy preformed as Cindy was in trouble with some important people and had to perform well or leave town. She said that people were glad she was going to get punished and urged me to redden her ass but good. Wow, suddenly I had a lot of power over this naughty young lady.

After she arrived I immediately ordered her to stand in the corner. I informed her that tonight was all about punishing her and should she refuse anything people would hear about it, people she'd prefer didn't. With a lump in her throat she submissively said "Yes Sir."

I sat on a chair and inspected my evening's entertainment. "Remove your dress slave" I barked "and don't you dare look at my eyes for the rest of the evening."

She quickly removed her dress and put it in the closet, going back to the corner when she was done.

"Pull your panties down to your knees." I ordered. Slowly, almost fearfully, she pulled her sheer black panties down. As Cindy pulled her panties down, she exposed her lovely rounded ass cheeks. Wow what a spankable ass. "Take three steps back" I said. She did. "Now remove your panties and bend over and put your hands on the wall." She did.

"Spread your legs slave." She did with some hesitation. "Spread them further and don't even consider disobeying me." She spread her legs a couple of feet further. I was now able to see her lovely brown asshole and her pussy lips. I walked over for a closer look. She was shaved all the way from her pussy to her ass, only a few days of stubble was present at most and she had nice healthy pussy lips.

I could feel the blood surge into my cock. I took off my underwear and was now naked.

"Please don't hurt me sir. I'll be a good girl" she begged submissively.

I ignored her. "Go lay over the big chair with legs spread and with your hands spread your cheeks slave, I want to see more of that beautiful ass and pussy."

She obeyed and using her hands spread her ass cheeks.

"Young lady, you are beautiful. You have a fantastic pussy and ass. Stand up and take off your bra, I want to see your tits." I told her.

"What are you going to do to me sir?" She said looking down. I must say I was impressed, she was in a bad position but was remained composed, however she had not yet removed her bra.

"You are going to be my sex toy this evening young lady and I am going to punish you at will as well as enjoy you in any way I wish." I told her. "If you young lady are in anyway uncooperative, I will tell those that want to know."

"Please sir, I'll do whatever you want, I promise" she begged.

Her hands went behind her back and she unbuckled her bra. She let it down and I got the full view of her big, beautiful tits. Her areola were brown and about the size of a half dollar coin. I watched as her nipples became erect from the cool night air.

"I expect nothing but obedience from you from now on. Do you understand that slave" I said to her.

"Yes." she replied.

"Excuse me" I roared.

"Yes, sir" she quickly said.

"Now that we have an understanding, come lay across my lap. It's time for your first spanking of the evening and then we get on to other things...NOW!"

She hurried to me and hesitated for only a moment as she went to lay down on my lap as I sat on the couch.

"Put your pussy directly over my legs." I told her. Now her nice ass was in easy reach.

"Thirty to each ass cheek should be a good warm up" I told her as my hand reached back, ready to strike.

"Oh please, noooooooooooooo" she cried.

I chose her right ass cheek, the one closest to me, for the first volley, and using my hand I spanked her hard... *WHACK! WHACK! WHACK! BAM! BAM!*

Her ass cheeks jiggled as my palm went from cheek to cheek and she cried out with each blow. I watched with great satisfaction as her cheeks quickly got red. *SMACK! SLAP! SMACK! SLAP! SPANK!*

She struggled, moaned and cried out but didn't try to get up. "Would you like me to stop Cindy? You know what will happen if I do."

She whimpered, "No sir, please don't stop."

I started to smell pussy juice. I pulled her ass cheeks open and could see her pussy was getting lubricated, hmmm looks like she was getting turned on quite a bit.

WHAP! SPANK! BAM! WHACK! SPANK!

It was great to watch her lying across my lap, her bare bottom already red. The smell of her wet pussy was a nice touch.

"Are you ready for the paddle young lady?" I asked sarcastically.

"Oh no" she cried, "Please no sir"

"You have such a spankable bare bottom. It will be tough for me to stop spanking you." *SPANK! WHAP! SPANK!*

"Spread your cheeks for me slave" I ordered her as I ran my fingers over her now red bare bottom.

She obediently reached back with trembling hands and spread her burning red ass cheeks. Reaching onto the small table beside me, I got some lubricant.

"Keep your cheeks spread. Should they stop being spread at anytime without permission, you will be in so much trouble young lady" I firmly told her. I heard a quiet sob as she dug her nails into her ass cheeks to keep them spread open wide. Her brown, wrinkled anus was a very inviting sight.

I lubricated my middle finger. Once it was well lubricated, I put my right hand between her legs and my left hand on her back. I leaned forward and gently caressed each of her lovely pussy lips.

My slave for the evening gasped, but did not move. I took exceptional delight in watching her anus flex uncontrollably as I caressed and teased her labia. Her body was reacting on its own to my playful touches. I could see the lips of her pussy becoming plumper from the anticipated invasion. I pushed my index finger between her lips and felt the hard little button of her clit. I heard her gasp.

As I continued to massage her clit, I let my lubricated middle finger rest against her anus and the other fingers against the inside of her right ass cheek. I started to flick my finger harder and faster across her clitoris and she started to uncontrollably pant.

"You have 15 seconds to start cumming from this slave but if you move from your position I will very, very severely punish you." I told her as my right index finger now rubbed against her clit harder and harder.

Cindy tensed and then began to orgasm. I was glad to see her cum. I was still going to beat her plenty more but I wanted her to love being forced to obey me. I planned on this being a very long evening for both of us.

Cindy cried out as she came, her ass cheeks and thighs straining to remain open, I could see the muscles in her back twitch as she came.

"Stay in position slave or I'll make your tits as red as your ass." I said sternly.

I took my index finger away from her clit and watched her shudder. Her pussy lips were completely open.

I started to massage around her anus with my middle finger. Once her asshole was slick with lubricant, I began to massage her anus with my middle finger, gently probing the edges and the entrance to her ass, but not penetrating.

"Please, not my ass" she begged.

"What?" I said.

"Please, not my ass, Sir." She said.

"Now you're just being funny" I said with a smirk. Wow how nice it was having a sex slave for the evening.

I said nothing but continued to massage her anus. Cindy didn't squirm but periodically I could feel her anus tense and relax. Soon though the sphincter muscles fully relaxed.

Without notice I penetrated her ass with my big middle finger. I curved my finger up and could feel her tailbone. My slave girl gasped once again.

I continued to explore her rectum with my middle finger. I'm not sure if it was fear or sexual ecstasy, or a combination of both but she was moaning hard with pleasure.

Now, I changed direction and pressed down toward her pussy, searching for her G-spot.

She let out a guttural scream as I found her G-spot and I used my thumb to play with her clit as I also probed her G-Spot through her anus. I made her cum again.

Cindy sighed as I removed my fingers, but I wasn't done with her ass yet. I took out a butt plug and inserted it, making her cringe.

"Young lady, if this butt plug comes out without my permission, I will whip your tits with my belt"

"Oh god, please no sir" she said suddenly scared.

I then took a paddle and once again the spanking onslaught continued. *SPANK! SPANK! SPANK! SPANK! SPANK!* She cried out but was careful to keep the butt plug in. *WHAP! BAM! SMACK! SMACK!* I now started spanking fast and hard, the hardest and fastest of the night.

"I dare you to move away slave. I just dare you." That stopped her fighting and her bare bottom would stay in place for the rest of the onslaught. *"Owwww, Ahhhhh, pleaseee sir."* Her ass which had lost some of its redness while I played with her, got it all back. It was once again the way a punished girl's ass should look, red and marked. I particularly enjoyed making the paddle land on the butt plug that was mostly buried in her ass.

I put the paddle down and once again fucked her ass with the butt plug, enjoying her moans. "Soon it will be my cock in there, not just a butt plug."

I told her to get up, which she did slowly, as the experience was draining her physically.

I sat on the edge of the bed and she knelt in front of me so she could suck on my cock. After 10 minutes of that I could take no more without cumming and told her to get on the bed on her hands and knees.

Well you can guess what happened next, I took her in her pussy and then her ass, thus concluding another great Las Vegas spanking memory.

5. October 15th, Tracy – Tracy answer my online ad. We chatted online but I thought she was too bitchy so I wrote her that I wasn't interested in her. Two days later she writes back and apologizes for giving the wrong impression. She also wrote that I could take it out on her butt. Well that's all I needed to hear. Just to play it safe I arranged for us to meet at a casino salad bar for dinner.

Unfortunately I once again sensed that she wasn't really into getting a good spanking but just curious, and wanted the money. My experience was that for the hardcore spanking I wanted to do, girls that are just curious wouldn't get through it. So I later excused myself.

6. October 24^h, Ginny – Well I had heard a former girlfriend that I had lived with had moved to Vegas some years back but I had misspelled her last name so I couldn't find her. One morning while I was fresh from sleep I suddenly remembered her last name's spelling. Hopefully she hadn't re-married and was using that same last name. As luck would have it she hadn't and we made contact.

We talked some on the phone and decided to meet for dinner. When I finally saw her I was concerned. She had lost 10-15 pounds and her breasts were Bs instead of the Cs I lived with. Bs are good though. She still had that schoolgirl look and worn a low cut dress. She looked tired and maybe not well bathed. However she seemed like the same nice person that unfortunately had fallen on hard times.

She explained how she had recently lost her job, car and roommate. Her credit was shot from less than frugal spending.

I asked her why she stopped writing me and she said from shame. She hadn't taken care of business as well as she should have in life.

"When you and I were together, thanks to your rules, accountability and discipline, I had direction in life which was so good for me. I went from living with my ex-husband who wouldn't hesitate to beat my ass with his belt to you who also kept me in line the same way."

We had lived together for several years and as I listened I could tell where it was going.

"You set limits for me, and when I exceeded those limits you punished me. I never realized how good for me that was."

I would spank Ginny often. Spanking was for foreplay and harder spankings were for discipline. I always had remembered all the hot discipline sessions we had. She was right, those sessions did her a world of good and I always wondered how things would be for her when she got transferred to the east coast by her company.

"You showed me that you cared and loved me by soundly spanking my bare bottom." She looked up at me with questioning eyes, "are you still a spanker?"

"With all my heart and soul" I answered knowing how badly she longed for a good, hard spanking.

She sat silently for several seconds took a deep breath and said. "Tom, I think what I need is for you to give me a good hard bare bottom spanking, would you please do that?"

I was not surprised by the request as I knew her well enough, and knew she needed it badly. "I would be happy to and I know that's just what you need."

Dinner was over soon and I drove us back to my place. I informed her that she would do exactly what I told her to do for the rest of the evening, which she agreed to. I had her take a shower and brought out her old schoolgirl outfit for her to wear. Amazingly I still had it. She thought that was great. She put it on though it was a bit loose.

I told her to bring a cushion over and kneel down in front of me and that he could no longer speak unless she's spoken to. The evening's discipline would now commence.

Her white schoolgirl dress shirt was buttoned up and she was wearing the bra she came here with.

She looked up at me longingly which was sweet but she would not be allowed to look up without permission. I reminded her of that and she apologized. I cut her slack as it had been so long that we last had a discipline session.

I then proceeded to chew her out for her undisciplined behavior. It made her cry. She repeated that the only way for her to get her act together is with discipline and she can't be allowed to get away with acting the way she had in the past.

I removed her white schoolgirl dress shirt and her bra and played with her tits as I scolded her. Her nipples were still sensitive and she moaned with my touch.

Wow, it was so nice to see a pretty girl that so desperately wanted a good long hard bare bottom spanking. Actually I could hardly believe my good fortune! But back to Ginny.

"Tonight young lady will be a night you will always remember because this begins our new journey together, a journey that will see you be all you can be." She felt very moved and while keeping her eyes down thanked me. I leaned down and gave her a long kiss which made her moan. While I was kissing her I reached down with both hands and massaged her asscheeks. They were warm from the shower but soon would be downright hot.

I pulled her hands up to my lap and tied them together. There was fear and anticipation in her eyes.

I then looked down at her and said "the time has come young lady, get over my lap." She looked scared but obeyed by laying over my lap with her head on my left.

I was prepared too. Next to me on the right side were a number of paddles, straps and sex toys.

"You should feel free to cry young lady as this is going to be as hard and as long a bare bottom spanking as I've ever given you." With that I brought a paddle down with moderate force. She exhaled and clinched her creeks.

"Sir" she said, "I haven't been spanked in a long time." "Well then we'll make up for lost time" I said reassuringly.

Ginny swallowed feeling a lump in the back of her throat. She felt strange but she liked that he cared and wanted to help her deal with her lack of discipline. She knew he knew how to change her habits and disposition. Then suddenly she was thinking of something else. The spanking had begun and now she was thinking of only one thing, the pain on her bare bottom.

SPANK! SPANK! SPANK! SPANK! SPANK!

Oh that's what a spanking feels like she thought, now I remember. Wow that's hurts but it was making her feel warm all over. *Finally a spanking!* She clasped a couch cushion and moaned progressively louder and louder. SPANK! SPANK! SPANK!

"During the spanking, when you're really sorry about the way things have been lately, I want you to apologize for letting it happen." "Yes sir" she whimpered. SPANK! SPANK! SPANK! SPANK! SPANK!

"Owwwwww, ohhhhhhh, I'm sorry sir." "Good girl but you're going to need a lot more of a bare bottom spanking for things to start to sink in."

Her moans were now cries as I spanked a lot harder and faster with the paddle. I would not hold back. I had carte blanche to beat sense into this young lady and that was what I was going to do. Tonight she learns her lesson, Tomorrow she has trouble sitting.

Periodically Ginny would relax her feet but quickly cross them again as the pain of the blows reminded her why she was here. She wanted to put her hands on her bare bottom to try and rub some of the burning sensation away, but they were tied in front of her. She tried gritting her teeth as he beat her tender behind. She started to pull her ass away but stopped when I threatened to start the spanking all over from the beginning, as well as spank her just as hard for the next 5 night in a row. Wow, five nights in a row, that would be a sexual sadist's dream come true, though I doubt if her butt could take it.

SPANK! WHAP! SPANK! WHACK! WHACK! *"Ohhhhhhh, owwwww, I'm sorry sir, please stop."*

I wasn't even thinking about stopping this spanking. The thought had not even crossed my mind. I would however take a rest at some point and have her stand in the corner in preparation for round two.

She was crying now, here cries were punctuated with each swat. Yes this bad girl was really learning her lesson.

"Oh god I'll be good I promise" she wailed kicking her feet. I was expecting the foot kicking so I stopped spanking long enough to put my right foot over her lower thighs to keep those in place.

I was impressed at how she still retained her ability to take a hard bare bottom spanking. Her submissive nature remained intact in many ways. I enjoyed the nostalgia of looking at an ex's well spanked bare bottom, one I hadn't seen in years.

SPANK! SPANK! SPANK! SPANK! SPANK! Then she tried to get up. "Even think about trying to get up again and all you get is the cane until I'm too tired to swing it." Hearing that made her scream. What a horrid thought. She would work harder at keeping in place. *Whap, Whap, Smack, Spank, Bam, Spank!* "Are you going to get your life in order young lady because I can do this to you every night" I secretly wished I could do this to her every night! *"Yessss sirrr. Owwwww."*

Her ass was mostly red and nicely marked. She was crying with real tears. Significant however was that I was tiring. The spanking would stop for now and she would spend sometime in the corner. I released my leg from over her legs. "Get up and kneel in front of me." She fell over my lap and quickly knelt in front of me trying so hard to rub her tender bare bottom but could barely reach them with her tied hands. As she sniffled I reached down and massaged and kneaded her well spanked cheeks. "Remember you have been ordered not to speak unless spoken to" I reminded her.

As her bottom was already so well spanked, maybe a second one would not be advisable after all; well the second one can be lighter.

Playing with her ass calmed her down some, now it was time to play with her breasts. I lifted myself up some and made myself at home with her breasts and their now firm nipples. Her sniffling was slowing and being replaced with moans of pleasure. "Hands on my legs" I ordered and she eagerly put her hands high on my legs.

"Now suck on my cock."

Her eyes were on it the whole time and she eagerly began sucking.

Unfortunately I was so turned on that I couldn't hold my orgasm back and soon filled her mouth with my cum. Fortunately she still remembered the importance of sucking down every drop of a man's cum.

Having orgasmed, I lost a good deal of my sexually sadist desires for the night. I let her go with just that spanking (though it was a nasty one.) I took her in her pussy and ass later that night and she moved in with me two weeks later. I'm happy to say that she is doing great and so am I.

My wonderful Las Vegas spanking adventure had a great ending. Wow about yours?

End

Bed Arrest, the Punishment For BDSM Enthusiasts

By Phil G.

Copyright (C) 2013

Trust, care, mutual consent, safe sex practices, and general safety are absolute priorities. No matter what it's suggested that you incorporate at least the following into your playtime and lifestyle:

* Don't tie things around someone's neck, and no breath play, period!
* Create a "Safe word" for the submissive to say when (or if) things get too scary.
* Always be careful and take necessary safety precautions when engaging in BDSM activity. Keep proper medical facilities handy.
* Always insure that a bound person has adequate circulation. If the person tied up has to go to the bathroom or has physical problems, that person must be immediately released from bondage.
* Ask about medical issues before playing and adjust your playing activities according to any medical issues.
* Never leave anyone bound and alone.
* Understand what a gagged person sounds like in sexual ecstasy versus in pain.
* Do not play while under the influence of drugs or alcohol.
Always check that your handcuffs and/or lock keys work before playing. If you have to go to the locksmith to get the handcuffs off, it's going to be embarrassing.
* When removing someone from bondage, allow them to move their own limbs.
* If pregnant or ill, check with your doctor before engaging in BDSM related activity.
* Always play within your own skill base and comfort level.

Defining Bed Arrest

Thank you for reading this book, the first book on bed arrest.

This punishment technique can only be used when all parties involved have fully consented to it.

For consistency's sake, this book discusses bed arrest where the punisher is a male master and the person being sentenced to bed arrest is a female submissive or slave. Bed arrest as a punishment can however work just as well in situations when the two parties involved are of the same sex.

I am honored to say that as a master I have incorporated bed arrest into my relationships many times. I have found that it can be a useful tool for changing errant sub/slave behavior.

In this book I'll also make suggestions regarding how (in my opinion) to most optimally carry out the sentence of bed arrest on a sub/slave. Obviously both parties involved can adapt what's in this book to fit their desires, needs and time schedule.

This book also assumes (for all involved) that the sub/slave will accept being put in bed arrest and obey her master's rules associated with it. Obviously if master tells his sub/slave she's just been sentenced to 10 hours house arrest and she points at him and laughs, then master has a problem.

General Definition - Bed arrest is when a master in a BDSM (or related) relationship orders (thus requires) his sub/slave to stay on her bed at all times other than emergencies, and for those additional activities specified. During the time that she is reprimanded to the bed, master may also punish her in other ways such as spanking. He can also play with her, and of course enjoy her sexually.

Bed arrest, as is obvious, is a lot like an adult version of timeout. It doesn't need to be for a longtime; a 30 minute bed arrest session might get the point across just as well. Still all bed arrests sessions are not the same and the sub's restrictions during her incarceration can make all the difference in the world. However beware guys, with her helplessly stuck there, will you be able to resist playing with her all afternoon? (Let's hope she doesn't consider that punishment.)

During bed arrest her freedom can be seriously restricted and she will have time to think about the importance of changing her errant ways.

I gave many 2 day sentences as well as 30 minute sentences. The longest bed arrest sentence I ever given a sub/slave was 4 days. On many occasions I commuted the sentence down because of good behavior, and/or something unexpected came up and/or her sexy begging finally got to me.

Bed arrest in and of itself might not be considered that extreme a punishment. The liberties that the sub/slave loses during bed arrest as well as other punishments she might also experience during that time perhaps can better determine how well she learns her lesson.

1. When to use bed arrest as a punishment. Perhaps your lovely lady has not been reacting well enough to your usual punishments. Perhaps spanking her used to work well as a punishment but now she gets so turned on by it that if anything she'll misbehave to get a good spanking. Finding a new punishment thus has become a necessity.

2. Length of time for putting the sub/slave in bed arrest. Obviously this varies by what extent she needs to be punished and what her and her master's obligations in life are during that time. (Does she have to go to work? Does she have college classes, etc.?)

As she will be allowed out of the bed (and home) for work and other responsibilities, likely that would mean an increase in the length of her sentence as she would be spending less time in bed arrest overall than a sub/slave that could stay around the home all or most of the day.

My experience (and yours may be quite different) is that if the sub/slave has never served a bed arrest, she may have fantasies associated with it.

3. What the sub/slave is allowed to do during bed arrest – How strict and restrictive will her sentence be, at least for the first half or so? Will she need permission to leave the bed for any reason (with the obvious exception of emergencies) including going to the bathroom?

The general rule of thumb is that the less you allow her to do during bed arrest, the more effective the punishment. During the sentence master can progressively give her back more privileges, such as no longer needing permission to go to the bathroom, watch TV, play videogames, watch movies, read books, use the phone, etc. Also was she tied to the bed at all times? Maybe now she can be unbound. (I would strongly suggest that except for emergencies she is never allowed to use the phone during bed arrest.)

My experience is that it's best to start the bed arrest with her having as few privileges as possible and being bound securely to the bed. You then give privileges back as she earns them and/or begs enough for them.

As it's likely you will let her out of the bed to fix meals and do other chores, you'll then need to make sure she's not taking unusually long to do those activities. If so master may want to threaten her with extending her sentence or perhaps another good spanking will take care of that problem.

4. Bondage and blindfolding during her incarceration. Will she be tied up and/or tied to the bed in bondage for a significant amount of the sentence? I would suggest she is and for a substantial amount of time, at least in the first half or more of her incarceration. Blindfolds can help make her feel more isolated and increase the impact of the punishment. Master will probably want to tie her hands in manner so that she **can't** take the blindfold off when she thinks master is not looking, or at least lower the blindfold a bit to look around real quick. Obviously a respectful, well trained sub/slave should not do this but sub/slaves are after all human.

5) Sub/slave needing permission from her master to leave the bed for anything (other than emergencies.) It may seem harsh but my experience is that bed arrest as a punishment works best when to leave the bed for even essential activities, such as going to the bathroom, the sub/slave first needs to have permission from her master. Because of this the master will find that he will need to be in the dwelling and at earshot at all times, just incase, which obviously could be inconvenient for him. With good behavior on her part, this restriction can be lessened.

6) Master will always determine what she does or doesn't wear during the period of bed arrest. *(This is of course is subject to how cold it is, if company shows up and/or if she has to go out of the house for work or other essential activities.)*

During bed arrest, while in private, it's suggested that she not be allowed to wear any clothing.

During the period of her incarceration, also perhaps remove her authority to wear panties while she is out of the house/apartment doing essential public activities such as work and shopping. *(Don't be surprised if she won't go along with this, particularly if it entails doing this at work. If that's the case guys, let it go.)*

7) Pouting, sulking and possibly rebelling by the sub/slave. Master should prepare for his sub/slave to possibly pout, sulk, and as a lengthy sentence progresses, maybe even try to rebel, though hopefully without going too far. Of course the more time master spends with her in bed, playing with her, spanking her, taking her being massaged by her, lying in bed with her, the happier she'll likely be but perhaps the punishment will be less effective, (or perhaps it could have just the opposite effect and be of good benefit).

It's possible that she will rebel to the point that she says she hates you and leaves the house frustrated. It is her right guys and you can't stop her, unfortunately it's likely also a sign of problems in the relationship, and/or a poorly trained sub/slave and/or a sub/slave that simply does not allow herself to be punished with bed arrest, (and/or perhaps other punishments you include during bed arrest.)

Still perhaps she has had a bad experience with bed arrest in the past? That will have to be dealt with in a responsible, respectful manner.

What if she doesn't like bondage and/or blindfolding then either she takes the plunge and lets you do that to her or you don't do those activities.

Perhaps she has obligations that she feels will interfere with the length of her sentence. You would need to let her off for those obligations anyway and perhaps she doesn't understand that.

On the other hand you as master might now find out that she is not a respectful sub/slave, an immature sub/slave and/or too much of a bratty sub/slave and you should find another.

8) Adding more time to her sentence as well as commuting her sentence. The sub/slave should be aware that more time can be added to her sentence. Additionally privileges might not be returned to her as fast during her sentence if she continues to be a bad girl and/or doesn't seem to be learning her lesson.

On the other hand, if she displays a respectful attitude and takes her punishment respectfully then the opposite can occur. Time can be taken off her sentence, and privileges can be returned more quickly during her sentence.

9. How often can we play while she is in bed arrest? Well guys, she's tied up to the bed, naked and blindfolded, good luck keeping your hands off of her! Still the master isn't the one being punished here so his needs and pleasure shouldn't suffer. If he wants his sub/slave to massage him, she should massage him. If he wants fellatio from his sub/slave, by all means get it. If he wants to take his slave, by all means take her. Still it breaks the monotony for her which might not be as conducive to punishment. But it will likely will give her pleasure, make her feel more wanted and loved. Hopefully that won't interfere with her learning her lesson and it might in fact help. Perhaps playing with her later during her incarceration is the better choice, if the master can hold out that long.

Hopefully throughout her sentence she will be on her best behavior in an attempt to get her sentence reduced.

10. What activities can the sub/slave do while she is in bed arrest?

A) Of course her work and parental responsibilities are fully allowed. (If you're living with kids, as you can imagine this punishment could be difficult to perform.)

Still master must watch to make sure she doesn't spend more time than she ordinarily would with her responsibilities. When that's the case her master may wish to add time to her incarceration and/or punish her in other ways.

B) She is required to satisfy her master's sexual desires as always as well as any other activities that can be performed on the bed that she would ordinarily do for her master. This includes massaging her master.

C) Her master perhaps may still also want to punish her in one or more other manners.

11. Privileges that can be taken away from the sub/slave during bed arrest include (depending on circumstances):

*Being able to enjoy video entertainment such as playing video games, watching videos, TV, movies, etc. That can include her favorite programming that would come on during her period of incarceration. (It can be recorded to be watched after her sentence is over.)

*Being able to talk (unless there is an emergency) or she needs permission to do something.

*Being able to use the phone.

*Being able to write things by hand.

*Being able to read for entertainment, such as books.

*Being allowed to have orgasms or otherwise pleasure herself (but dude that's harsh!)

12. Do you close the door on her during her confinement?
No, but it's the master's choice if she's allowed to look at him.

13. How to react to her begging during incarceration. If your sub/slave is adept at begging and if they can be real sexy while doing it, masters may have to ban begging during bed arrest altogether or deal with the horniness that comes with it.

I for one like it when she begs and you can require a certain number of "begs" from her before you'll even consider commuting her sentence.

14. Additional punishments while she is in bed arrest. Perhaps you would like to give her "hourlies". These are spankings given every hour during a set period. She needs to make sure that her master knows it is time for her hourly spanking (or other prescribed hourly punishment) or risk having addition time added to her sentence.

15. Additional general advice to the master. Guys you need to hold strong and be firm. That can be tough. Make sure she takes you seriously throughout this period.